WHO ARE YOU
AND
HOW DO YOU KNOW?

Identifying with the Inner ME

Written by Marie Mouzon

For the Young and Old alike

Who ARE YOU
and
HOW DO YOU KNOW?
Identifying with the Inner ME

*A Journal and Explanation of the Five-Fold Gifts
given by Christ*

Written by Marie Mouzon

For the young and old alike

Table of Contents

FORWORD

Sit down, fasten your seatbelt and take an enjoyable ride as you read this masterful presentation that begins with a significant--universal question, "Who are you; and, how do you know?" There seems to be an allusion that if you get it wrong, there will be an inner conflict that can only be satisfied by the correct answer.

These questions have been raised by each of us. Some have inquired for spiritual reasons, others for physical or natural reasons; all of which affect us emotionally. Amidst an age of identity theft and identity crises, we are required to emphatically know, who we are. No matter how effective many seem to be in re-creating themselves, it is my opinion that we can only be happy in being who we were created to be. Otherwise, life is unfulfilling, frustrating, and often apathy sets in.

When the natural connects with the spiritual, an eternal combustion takes place within us that releases both fusion and fission, spontaneously. Resultantly, who we become, makes us capable of being functional and effective in multiple realms of life. We are capable of doing well in the nuclear church, where we gather, and in the extended church, where we scatter to live, work and play.

However, our natural propensity is not to ask, "Who am I?" We are more apt to ask, "What can I do?" Consequently, we are more apt to "do" than we are to "be." Life teaches us to do, how to do, and defines for us what it is to do well. Now we are likewise being challenged to consider, "who" we are before we agree to "do." Though the answer is thought to be evasive, each of us can know "who we are."

In this book, Marie Mouzon offers us an eternal solution. Though it is not a one-size-fit-all, there is a-size-for-all. She presents to us our availability to who Christ was when He was in the earth, and how He left himself as five gifts to us, so that we can be who He was. She uses Ephesians 4: 8, 11-13 as a baseline for us to grasp this great truth. Not only does she identify these gifts to the church as Christ ascended to His Father, but she also discusses their functionality, their purpose, and their consummation. The practicality of the book will be useful for students of all ages. Small groups, in particular, will find great reward in sharing the different chapters. I foresee others dramatizing the five gifts to make learning fun.

We refer to these gifts as five-fold ministries. These gifts are not meant to be esoteric. Any leader in the Body is eligible as one of these gifts. Though three of them, evangelists, pastors and teachers, are most popular, there is a need to embrace the apostle and prophet, as well. The lack of either gift leaves the Body desperate. It takes all five to perfect the saints, for their work of ministry, so that the Body of Christ is built up.

The timeframe for the operation of these gifts is known by what gets accomplished. This is clear in Ephesians 4:12. The Body must bear witness of unity of the faith; knowledge of the Son of God; a perfect man; and, measuring up to the stature of the fullness of Christ. The rest of Ephesians 4 then clearly states what the results will be, i.e. there will be no more children of God tossed to and fro, and carried about with every wind of doctrine, etc.

This book is a must read for emerging leaders, churches and ministries that lack strong leadership. If church growth has alluded you, this book can be a useful tool. Get started by asking the big question, "who am I; and, how do I know?"

Enjoy your adventure.

Your Kingdom Servant,

++ Ralph L. Dennis

ACKNOWLEDGEMENTS

Well, we are finally here. This is the first among many books that reside in my belly.

First, I would like to thank the Holy Spirit for allowing me to pen what has been inside of my heart for so long.

I would also like to acknowledge and express my LOVE to my Dad, Burnice Jackson and my Mom, Jean Jackson who are no longer with us but have deposited powerful nuggets in me. They are two of the greatest people I have ever known. I love you both forever.

Next, I would like to thank my Spiritual Father, Archbishop Ralph Dennis, for teaching me about the Five-Fold Ministry Gifts. So even now, I don't think I am crazy. Thanks Dad.

My gratitude also goes to my two daughters who keep me grounded and never let me forget who I am in the Body of Christ. Also to my five grandbabies "Maxwell, Raven, Elijah, Dylan and Mekhi" who I love with all of my heart, and I am determined to make sure they walk fully in who Christ has called them to BE.

I would also like to thank some very dear friends "They know who they are" who talked me through this journey and kept me from giving up so many times. Our Sister/Friend love cannot be touched.

This one touches me deeply, to my Beloved Husband who I have been with since I was 17 years old. You are God's joy to me and I love how you love me. Thank you for always believing in me and always treating me like a Queen.

INTRODUCTION

There is a part of ourselves that many have not tapped into yet. I say YET because this book is going to help us Identify with the Inner ME, that person no one told us about. Note: Every good and perfect gift comes from above. (James 1:17 KJV) So strap on your seat belts as we expose the hidden treasures God has placed in each of us.

In this complex and evil world, I have come to the conclusion that we MUST prepare our babies and young children for battle. Battle with whom, and against what you say? Battle with the evils of this world and against the disillusions that have secretly and many times boldly confronted each of us, even as children. "Wherein in time past ye walked according to the course of this world, according to the prince of the power of the air, the spirit that now worketh in the children of disobedience." (Ephesians 2:2 KJV)

The objective here is to understand and also teach our children to use the gifts that God has given each of us "Boldly and Unapologetically." As we walk through these guidelines, instructions and examples, just remember they are simply written that you might come to an understanding of who you are before the enemy (devil) tells you who you are. Even though he is a liar from the beginning, (John 8:44 KJV) "Ye are of *your* father the devil, and the lusts of your father ye will do. He was a murderer from the beginning, and abode not in the truth, because there is no truth in him.

When he speaks a lie, he speaks of his own: for he is a liar and the father of it". The Bible tells us that the enemy comes to Kill, Steal, and Destroy. (John 10:10 KJV) Be aware and be on watch.

Every setback, struggle, disappointment, wrong turn, or mishap was designed to make us think we have failed. It is the enemy's plan to kill your vision, dreams, purpose, and to steal your opportunities, hopes, plans, and MOST OF ALL to destroy YOU and everything God purposed for you to Execute, Release, and Accomplish. "When you know your Identity in Christ, no devil in hell can take that away from you, not even the enemy of our own souls.

It has been quoted "Knowledge is power." (Bacon, Francis, 1597) and I am in agreement that the more you understand and know who God called you to be, the enemy has less ability to tell you who you ARE NOT. "My People perish for the lack of Knowledge." (Hosea 4:6 KJV) We are in a very strange time in our lives, a time that no one has ever seen before, and as the Bible has stated "These are signs of the last days. (Matthew 24 KJV), and I believe that being equipped and assured of your dominion and authority you are at a better advantage to live a life of victory, even at a young age.

My Spiritual Father, Archbishop Ralph L. Dennis has coined this phrase "I BE who God say I BE, I BE that now and nothing else."

At the early ages starting as young as three years old we should be making this declaration so at a timely age we can learn to defend our faith, as well as walk in the Authority where with Christ has made us FREE.

Chapter One

Each of us has been given a Special Set of Skills (Gifts) to overthrow, overtake, and annihilate the plans and schemes of the devil in our lives and the lives of others. The promise from God is that He has given us power over all the powers of the enemy and nothing by any means shall harm us. (Luke 10:19 KJV) The Bible also tells us that "According as his divine power hath given unto us all things that pertain unto life and godliness, through the knowledge of him that hath called us to glory and virtue." (2 Peter 1:3 KJV) If we can educate, prepare, endorse and provoke the people of God at the tender ages of three and above, I believe there will be a Generation that God will raise up "but the people who do know their God shall be strong, and do great exploits." (Daniel 11:32 KJV)

Let us identify who the enemy really is "For we do not wrestle with flesh and blood, but against principalities, against powers, against rulers of the darkness of this age, against spiritual hosts of wickedness in the heavenly places." (Ephesians 6:12 KJV), so we will not destroy one another in our Pursuit to "Find Ourselves" These spirits look like "doubt, fear, confusion, anxiety, unbelief, lies, defeat, perversion, hate, unforgiveness, depression, rejection, selfishness, pride, neglect, greed, envy, etc." I'm sure you can name a few.

"Who are you and how do you know?"

This dialogue is designed to help identify and bring out the secrets or hidden gifts and talents that our babies, young people and adults are struggling to make sense of as they walk through their identity crisis. Hopefully each of you will grab nuggets from any part of this book. It is written for the young and the old, sometimes adults need the simplicity as if they were a child. "Verily I say unto you, whosoever shall not receive the kingdom of God as a little child, he shall not enter therein." (Mark 10:15 KJV)

Let's take a look at this Power Scripture that the Lord gave us to set balance to our dimensional identity.

Ephesians 4:8-13 KJV "Wherefore he saith, when he ascended up on high, he led captivity captive, and gave gifts unto men. (Now that he ascended, what is it but that he also descended first into the lower parts of the earth? He that descended is the same also that ascended up far above all heavens, that he might fill all things.) And he gave some Apostles; and some Prophets; and some Evangelists; and some Pastors and Teachers; For the perfecting of the saints, for the work of the ministry, for the edifying of the body of Christ: Till we all come in the unity of the faith, and of the knowledge of the Son of God, unto a perfect man, unto the measure of the stature of the fullness of Christ."

We have also been blessed with gifts of the Spirit by the Holy Spirit (I Corinthians 12:4 KJV)

Word of Wisdom

Word of Knowledge

Faith

Gifts of Healing

Working of Miracles

Prophecy

Discerning of Spirits

Divers (or different) kinds of Tongues

Interpretation of (different) Tongues

(1 Corinthians 12:8-10 KJV)

These scriptures are considered Power Scriptures, because they have a single thought in mind and that is to remind each of us that we were brought with a high price and our callings are secured in what Christ has accomplished for us. The goal here is that We would all come to the unity (oneness) of heart or belief and the intentional consistent concept that we were made in the Image and after the Likeness of God, (Genesis 1:26 KJV) and that is what we are to BE in fullness in the earth, consequently this must ring forever in our hearts and minds.

Many, if not most of us in the entire world, and this crosses racial and social boundaries, struggle with "Who We Are" due to the many facets of life. I believe as in the very beginning, the earth was cursed and as a result, countless spirits were released such as FAILURE, LOW-SELF ESTEEM, HATRED, MURDER, ENVY, STRIFE, and many, many more. Therefore, it is of the utmost importance to know who God made us to be, and to keep reminding ourselves that our gifts will make room for us (Proverbs 18:16 KJV). We must remind ourselves and others as much as possible that we are Fearfully and Wonderfully Made by God. (Psalm 139:14 KJV) and we are not who our situations and circumstances say we are. We are victorious in every area of our lives. I also must remind us that Iron does indeed sharpen Iron. (Proverbs 27:17 KJV)

According to the Scriptures, let's look into the GIFTS that Jesus gave us as He ascended on high, and what these gifts will look like as we develop from children to adults.

Chapter Two

APOSTLE ~~ PROPHET ~~ EVANGELIST ~~

PASTOR ~~AND TEACHER

As a young child, I had visions and dreams. Many times my dreams would come to pass in one way or another. The one dream I had of King Kong taking over the Subway Station in New York City didn't come true, thank God, (smile) however, I could see a pattern or a way I believe God spoke to me through visions and dreams. Even though my childhood was peculiar, or some would note it as weird, I also had an overwhelming desire to see people happy and free. Happy because most of the time I was sad, and free because I felt like I was locked in a crazy, dysfunctional situation and could not get out. So many times, we shut down as children because of fear and the biggest possibility is that no one would believe us. I was hearing things while I was asleep and while I was awake. I was also seeing open visions but of course didn't know what to do with it all. I wondered sometimes if I was crazy, or maybe I wasn't and everyone else was. Many times as a child, I wrote poetry and I expressed myself by writing. Even if I was expressing anger, fear or disappointment, I found comfort in hiding away and writing. My dreams were so real sometimes I would wake up crying and sweating. It was exciting and sometimes very scary. The problem was no one would listen. Dreams can sometimes become nightmares if we are not careful.

If you can recall when we were children, someone would ask us "What do you want to be when you grow up?" We still of course ask that same questions today. Well, I always wanted to be a preacher (I believe because my Grandmother was a preacher, and even though I was mad at God, I still believe in my heart that God and I had something special.) However, my life and behavior certainly didn't look like I was headed in that direction (smile). There were other ideas of becoming other things, but thank God, He had other plans for my life. There were secret traps and pitfalls set up to take me off course. I could hear it screaming at me that I would be nothing, and would always be a failure, "I would always be like my (natural) father." My focus was driven by my pain of rejection, abuse and disappointments. This is one of the reasons this book is so important to me because it seemed like there was no one to help me out of my darkness, despair and confusion. My family and others around me couldn't even help themselves.

I felt powerless to help myself so I was SCREAMING from within (CAN ANYONE HEAR ME????) Yet, it seemed like no one understood. Nevertheless, I had an earnest desire to rescue (liberate) others. I just wanted to help, and this I knew for sure was a part of my makeup. I always wanted to protect and nurture people, however because of my insecurities; I always wanted to do the hugging. I didn't trust others to hug me or love me. I remember as a child, around the ages of eight and ten, speaking with adults reassuring and consoling them while telling them that things would get better and trying to direct them when I didn't know how to direct myself. What was it that they saw in me? Me saying, "God loves you and wants more for you," when I didn't even trust God to protect me. I was confused, however when the opportunity presented itself for me to speak something edifying, it just came out. This reminds me of the scripture: For we are God's masterpiece. He has created us anew in Christ Jesus, so we can do the good things he planned for us long ago. (Ephesians 2:10 KJV)

I didn't have the safest, or the best nurturing environment or upbringing (that's my other book), but I knew there was something about me that was special. It's hard to comprehend when you are living with people who cannot identify the special gifts that are within you or even know how special they themselves are. Here's a side bar (one of many), If we can protect, empower, and speak volumes to our children while they are still babies, we would be assured to have a functional and thriving generation that would Not Kill, but LOVE one another and esteem others higher than themselves (Philippians 2:3 KJV). If we taught this in schools and talked about these gifts and talents around the dinner table, we would have less bullying and suicide at such young ages. I JUST BELIEVE GOD.

Chapter Three

Let me share my thoughts as we move forward in this writing to gather the concepts of our connection to Who we are and Who God said we are to BE.

Before the beginning of our lives, the Bible tells us that God Knew Us! "Before I formed thee in the belly I knew thee; and before thou came forth out of the womb I sanctified thee, and I ordained thee a prophet unto the nations." (Jeremiah 1:5 KJV)

Just like me, we were all born with wonderful gifts and talents. "Every good gift and every perfect gift is from above, and cometh down from the Father of lights, with whom is no variableness, neither shadow of turning." (James 1:17 KJV) These gifts were given to be used for the up building of the Kingdom of God. Whether you choose to use your gifts and talents is up to you, however, you will forego the ultimate design of God. "Be Fruitful, Multiply, Replenish, Subdue and HAVE Dominion." (Genesis 1:26 KJV), because they are not REFUNDABLE. For the gifts and calling of God are without repentance. (Romans 11:29 KJV) (SMILING) You can't give them back, and Trust me; God will get a return on His Investment. It was never God's plan for us to be defeated, or destroyed by the enemy. The Word of God declares "I've given you POWER to tread upon serpents and scorpions and over all the power of the enemy and nothing by any means shall harm you." (Luke 10:19 KJV) We were created to WIN, but you have to first understand your posture of VICTORY and <u>know who you were called to BE</u>. Not only know who you are, but understand your sphere (domain) of RULE.

This is written so that we won't lose our young people and to also infuse the older ones of their Greatness and Authority because of God's initial plan for each of us. I want to share with you that you MUST at all cost, teach your three-year old children, and even younger, how to pray. Never negate the Power of prayer and faith. (I asked God and I believe God) This is not easy when what you prayed for didn't happen right away or how your mind told you, it would or should happen. I have found out that all things just don't happen in our time frame, God has the time frame already set, and we just have to walk into His timing. When you pray, share with your family what you are believing God for. Maybe just a little bit but when it comes to pass, and most times it will, you will be able to give that testimony so they too "Can Believe." I used to lay hands and pray for my family and friends because I saw my Grandmother do it when I was little. Crazy as it was, I really did believe God would heal.

I believe our goal here is to grab hold of these special gifts and talents at a young age so children/youth don't have to wait until they are 20 to 50 years old to optimize (get the most out of) the gifts given to them. Many kings and rulers in our Bible were ruling at a very young age. Some examples are (Joash was seven years old when he began to reign) (2 Chronicles 24 KJV), David was commissioned King at the age of 10. (1 Samuel 16:13 KJV)

Heretofore, as children we are challenged to know, understand, make sense of dreams, desires, passions, behaviors, etc. It is impossible to figure these experiences out because most of the time we do not have an idea of TRUTH until many years later. Then we can say Oh, this is what that meant.

Many children experience (seemingly) phenomenon's early in life and like me these strange experiences are not explained, or expounded upon. There are experiences such as dreams, visions, open visions, extreme urges to help, assist, and care for other people less fortunate than them (compassion). Also, we experience cravings for learning, knowledge, love of art, drawing/sketching, building. Other experiences show up like teaching others, feeling the desire to share what you have heard in your spirit, and desires to know more (believing there is more than meets the eye). Have you ever had a child tell you God said. or something told me? These are just some of the things that happen as we grow into the BE that God intended for us. Somewhere along the journey, you MUST realize that you are not strange, but Unique.

There were times, I'm sure, when you left people older than you scratching their heads. (laughing) The joy of writing this book fills me up because this is a universal cry, not just in your neighborhood. There are many just like you and me, the packaging might be different, but the results or goals are normally the same. *__We Rule__*

Chapter Four

Ok, how do you explain these wonders that happen or are happening in your child's life, as a matter of fact, happening in your own life right now as we are reading. As you are reflecting on your own past, the images are coming back to you. Images of times when you felt out of place, misunderstood, falsely accused, a loner, problematic, and the list goes on and on. It wasn't that you were any of those things. Your true GIFT was being over looked because people were unable to recognize in you, likewise even in themselves, that we are all created for much more than _______________ you can fill in the blank. I'm sure you can identify with some of the questions we've asked ourselves and others many times over, "Why was I born? What is my purpose in life? How do I find out who I am, etc.?" Consequently, many of our passions will lead us right to purpose. Many of the things we find ourselves drawn to will help guide us to purpose. Things such as our vocation, our occupation, our hobbies or interest are great places to begin when we try to find out WHAT, WHERE and WHY. There is a secret to our development, growth, and awareness, and that is to never try to measure up to someone else's development, growth, awareness, and gifts. You are unique, a designer's original. Your design is distinctive, your smile, your eyes, your walk, everything. Whether we realize it or not, our existence was designed to help someone else develop and grow. "STOP FIGHTING AGAINST IT."

Every now and then we have to STOP, take a deep breath, and EXHALE. We grow up with a million questions and thoughts about Why, When and Where. Our brains, (which I believe), is connected to our soul, is in a survival battle trying to fit into the world. Consequently, we will never fit in (smile). We are Great because God is Great. We just are "Period". Who can really argue with that statement?

I was taught, and I agree, that there are three dimension of each gift:

1) The spirit of

2) The gift of

3) The Office of

Let me explain, for example:

(The Spirit) If the major Spirit/flow in the house (church/ministry) is Prophetic, you are guaranteed to have your congregation receiving downloads from Heaven through that Spirit/flow.

(The Gift) if your Ascension Gift is Prophetic your gifting will flow profoundly in that area, and

(The Office) As you operate in your Ascension Gift, (the gifts Christ gave after He ascended), and you prefect it in maturity and growth, you will maintain a level of Proficiency in this area. (A Place of RULE)

Let's continue as we learn more about the Power of our Gifts and how we can utilize them for Christ Sake (In

Ministry, In the Marketplace, At Home, and Every day). These are some of the definitions:

<u>Apostle</u> – One sent by God, One commissioned (appointed) by Christ: Jesus Christ the Chief Apostle (i.e. As the Father sent his Son into the world) John 3:17 One who is given to order. The twelve Apostles were commissioned to make disciples of all nations (Matthew 28 KJV)

<u>Prophet</u> -- Foreseer, Forth teller, one who warns of Divine judgment upon sin, both Personal and National. (Hebrew-Nabi) (Numbers 12:6-8 KJV) One who hears from the Father and shares the Father's heart. "Good or Bad"

<u>Evangelist</u> – One who is given to share the glad tidings to those who have not known them. To carry the gospel to all the world and to share the good news. (2 Timothy 1:1, Acts 4:5 and Matthew 28) (i.e. Jesus Christ – Luke 20:1, Paul – Romans 1:15, Philip – Acts 21:8, Timothy – 2 Timothy 4:5 and all the other disciples who were instructed to "Go ye into all the world and Preach the Gospel to every creature (Mark 16:15 KJV)

<u>Pastor</u> – A Shepherd, (Greek: Poi men) One who instructs, teaches, and protects. One who has compassion for, to feed (Matthew 9:36 KJV)

<u>Teacher</u> – One who is enabled to effectively communicate the truths of the Bible to others. One who is gifted in explanation (1 Corinthians 12:28 KJV)

Chapter Five

Let's examine some behaviors that we have seen throughout the lives of our children:

what about the child who has been drawing and sketching/drawing since they were really young, or

the child who always brought kids home from school or from the neighborhood to feed them, or

the child who told you Sasha from my class is always hungry or wears dirty clothes "Mom can we help" or

what about that child who wakes with nightmares, dreams, having recurring dreams, visions.

Parents never really knew how to help or explain what was happening. Parents or relatives normally said the child was strange, or acting out.

what about your child that always appeared to be the leader in his or her group? Most times having a hard time with incompetence. This child appears to be very controlling, governing, and in charge.

what about the child who loved having their room and toys neat and took extra care to put things in order and seemed out of place being around confusion or chaos?

what about the child that feels they are different. They don't fit in with the other kids. Everyone thinks they are strange. They simply see things different or their interests are peculiar. (I think I like that word Peculiar)

what about the child who functions as extremely shy, withdrawn, reserved, introverted, and so on. They seem to only thrive or appear excited when they are in an artistic, imaginative, environment being in a resourceful mode. Wow! Where would you see this child in the future?

what about your child wanting to be a creative writer, dancer, singer, artist, and you identify these gifts but don't know how to address them or encourage them. This child might appear weird or strange because they feel empty or unfulfilled.

Let us learn to identify the gifts in our children and not just think them as odd. They are actually extraordinary. Each one of us are born with Ascension Gifts (Ephesians 4:11-13), and Spiritual Gifts (1 Corinthians 12:1-11 KJV)

Our children suffer because adults have not heretofore been able to identify with their own gifts and callings. As much as most of us have been taught Morals and Values, and other positive teachings we have experienced in our history, we struggled with lies, deceit, family secrets, and so on. It has become a revolving door for dysfunction. We do not know, our parents did not know and their parents did not know. How do we figure this all out? Please place in your heart and mind the desire to Know Who You Are by reading the Word of God (Holy Scriptures) and hearing "Who God say you BE". The dysfunction from the enemy would hope you never find out who you really are. Let me just give you a whisper; You are a Mighty Force in the

Earth and your purpose is to continue what Christ began before He went back to sit at the right hand of the Father. (John 14:12 KJV) "Christ came to destroy the works of the devil" (1 John 3:8 KJV), and don't worry God has given us everything pertaining to life and Godliness (2 Peter 1:3). Christ also gave us power over ALL the powers of the enemy – (Luke 10:19). I am sure I said that somewhere else in this book. (smile)

"There is a revelation through knowing Christ Jesus that affords us the opportunity to "Walk Out the Fullness of who Christ Purposed, and Destined us to truly BE"

Chapter Six

"Jesus the Apostle"

<u>The APOSTLE</u> – One sent by God, one commissioned by Christ.

We have also heard the five ministries in Ephesians 4:11 referred to as "ascension gift ministries," because Jesus gave them when he ascended. However, Ephesians 4:8 says that when Christ ascended, he gave "gifts to men," and "men" is used as a generic term for all Believers. We know this because it is defined in the preceding verse, which says, "To each one of us grace has been given." (Ephesians 4:7) So again, each Believer has a gift/s. These gifts were given due to the ascension of Jesus Christ, not just to a few select Believers. The epistles of Romans, Corinthians, and Ephesians, are all in agreement that each Believer has a "gift" ministry, a way of serving that is specifically given to him or her.

"And God hath set some in the church, first apostles, secondarily prophets, thirdly teachers, after that miracles, then gifts of healings, helps, governments, diversities of tongues. (I Corinthians 12:28)

The Apostle is one who functions in orderly operation, methodical, systematical, meticulous, and so on. An Apostle is a Foundation Layer. A person who by the leading of the Holy Spirit gives instructions and guidelines to make clear a strategic and well developed plan or strategy. The Apostle is an Atmosphere Shifter. The spirit of this person commands environment changes (if you will) and those in their sphere can feel the command in the room.

I have watched as children shift the atmosphere at the playground, classroom, home and not even realize that they were created to lead, control, and command. Many people call these types of children "bossy, controlling, conceited, and arrogant" they have even been falsely accused of having a bad attitude. They really don't have a bad attitude, they simply have an idea of how things are supposed to be situated in appearance or be situated for growth or movement.

Hard to explain, yet these types of children are branded as troublemakers, but really, they are atmosphere shifters. Apostles are in command. They are given to RULE, and if that is not your strength you become uncomfortable around someone who takes charge and lays foundations for change.

Let us look at some characteristics of The Apostle.

"Apostle" means a person who is sent to represent another—whether a king, kingdom or entity like a church. (1 Corinthians 12:28 KJV) teaches that God places first in the church apostles, since they are sent by God to lay foundation and to set order. (Just like Christ, who was sent by God) This is recognized as children are growing and identifying or finding their place in life. Apostolic characteristics sometimes show up in children who act out and need structural guidance. It appears that they are fighting against order or directives, however they are actually screaming out for it. Most children with this type of calling don't realize it but they are like a fish without water when there is no structure.

You identify this gift because at work, home or play, you will see the drive to bring something to life. Apostles operate best when leading, formulating plans of action and gravitating to others with the same flow. Many will look to dismantle confusion and begin navigating around a solution. As Apostles develop, the essential goal for them is to "Keep Building." What I love about the Apostolic Gift is that it can touch all of the other ascension gifts. The entire essence of Jesus can be seen by way of these individuals.

As you will begin to take notice, your ascension gifts are not given to us by man. Consequently, they are given to us by Christ. If we would only pay close attention to how we are wired, we will see the evidence of our gifts through our daily actions. One thing for sure, Apostles are known to affect some type of change wherever they are planted (school, home, work, church, communities, etc.).

Let us take the lead from our Leader "Jesus the Christ" He was indeed Sent by God (John 3:16 KJV) into the world because God loved us so much. Jesus being sent made him "The Chief Apostle." There is another scripture that suggests that we too have been sent into the world. "As my Father has sent me, even so send I you" (John 20:21 KJV) and of course (Matthew 28:18-20 KJV) "Go ye into all the world and make disciples." It would look as though we all have an Apostolic Work.

____

____

____

____

____

____

____

____

____

____

____

____

____

____

"Is this your gift? If not, keep reading."

Chapter Seven

"Jesus the Prophet"

The PROPHET--Foreseer, Forth teller, One who warns of Divine judgment upon sin, both personal and national. One who <u>hears</u> from the mouth of God and speaks what he/she has heard.

Just for your understanding, we read in the Bible that there are 17 Major and Minor Prophets spoken of in the Old Testament.

The Bible also says, "Surely the Lord GOD does nothing without revealing His secret plan [of the judgment to come] to His servants the prophets." (Amos 3:7 KJV)

The Major Prophets and Minor Prophets are simply a way to divide the Old Testament prophetic books.

The Major Prophets are Isaiah, Jeremiah, Lamentations, Ezekiel, and Daniel.

The Minor Prophets are Hosea, Joel, Amos, Obadiah, Jonah, Micah, Nahum, Habakkuk, Zephaniah, Haggai, Zechariah, and Malachi.

The Major Prophets were described as "Major" because their books are longer and the content has far-reaching, even worldwide effects.

The Minor Prophets were described as "Minor" because their books are shorter (although Hosea and Zechariah are almost as long as Daniel is) and the content is more narrowly focused.

This does not mean the Minor Prophets are any less inspired than the Major Prophets. It is simply a matter of how God chose to reveal more to the Major Prophets than He did to the Minor Prophets.

Where do dreams/visions come from?

Dreams - A dream is a succession of images, ideas, emotions, and sensations that usually occur during a full eight-hour night sleep. Most dreams occur in the typical two hours of REM (Rapid Eye Movement). How do you explain this when younger children experience dreams that cannot be comprehended.

How do we explain the mystery of children seeing, hearing and experiencing phenomenon's, at a young age?

What you know about yourself is about one ounce of information until you have been introduced to the Master of your fate. I know you have heard you are the Master of your own fate, but really, you do not have a clue. As a young child, even as young as 3 years old, children have been having dreams that they can recall, and remember. Of course, they are not descriptive in how they explain what they saw, but it normally comes out later on as they grow up. You ever heard of "The Imaginary Friend?" Well that is not altogether weird. It is normally identified as a coping mechanism. Something to keep the child company. I believe it is building the child's imagination as well as building a trusting relationship with someone/something. I know it did for me. I definitely had an Imaginary Friend. Many times prophets find themselves alone and isolated, feeling like they have no friends. When you operate with the gift of prophecy as a child, you will notice your child is very creative, musically inclined, inquisitive, gifted in storytelling, and so on. A lot of times, they are angry because they feel unnoticed, or isolated because they feel weird, and misunderstood. However, they are brilliant and most times see what others don't see. It is amazing how God allows the Holy Spirit to reveal some things at different times. Let's pay attention to our children because their minds are just like sponges. They absorb good and evil with what we allow them to be around. It definitely affects and effects their behavior. Consider to always guard your eye gate, what you watch, and ear gate, what you listen to. These are the major entranceways for the enemy.

____

____

____

____

____

____

____

____

____

____

____

____

____

____

"Is this your gift? If not, keep reading."

Chapter Eight

"Jesus the Evangelist"

The EVANGELIST – One who is given to share the glad tidings to those who have not known them.

"But watch thou in all things, endure afflictions, do the work of an evangelist, make full proof of thy ministry." (2 Timothy 4:5)

In the Mind of God, he gave two (2) Great Commandments:

"Thou shalt love the Lord thy God with all thy heart, and with all thy soul, and with all thy mind. This is the first and great commandment. (Matthew 22:35-40)

And the second is like unto it, Thou shalt love thy neighbor as thyself. (Mark 12:31) On these two commandments hang all the law and the prophets."

And, The Great Commission:

"Go ye therefore, and teach all nations, baptizing them in the name of the Father, and of the Son, and of the Holy Ghost: Teaching them to observe all things whatsoever I have commanded you: and, lo, I am with you always, even unto the end of the world. Amen." (Matthew 28:16-20 KJV)

This ministry gift happens to be one of my favorite because I believe that this is the heartbeat of Christ. The Bible says He came to seek and to save those that are lost.

(Matthew 18:11 and Luke 19:10 KJV) As you consider this gift, let us look at what it means: Everyone is born in the world as a sinner because of the first Adam's disobedience "The Fall" (Genesis chapter 3 KJV) The bible says "We were born in sin and shapen in iniquity (Psalm 51:5 KJV). Here's another scripture "For All have sinned and come short of the glory of God". (Romans 3:23 KJV) Here is one of My Favorite "For God so loved the world that He gave His only begotten Son that whosoever believeth in Him should not perish but have everlasting life." (John 3:16 KJV) Ok, one more, "When you are converted, strengthen your brother." (Luke 22:32 KJV)

Looking at this ministry gift reminds me of a LOVE so unexplainable that your heart and your soul are entrenched, wrapped together and bound by a Three-Fold Cord "Father, Son, Holy Spirit."

Also, I heard the voice of the Lord, saying, whom shall I send, and who will go for us? Then said I, Here am I; send me. (Isaiah 6:8 KJV) When you really examine all of the other gifts, we realize that in spite of the title given we are ALL required to GO.

God has always LOVED us and desired that we would come back to Him. Love Him more than ______________ (You add your distraction or thing that seems to come before GOD, or that has become an idol), (For example, your looks, your friends, your fears, your money, your clothes, your work, etc.)

I know in my lifetime I needed someone to save me from myself. The truth is, I didn't even know I needed a Savior until someone came to see about me. My distractions were my family, drugs, promiscuity, perversions, lies, anxieties, disappointments, depression, feeling isolated, rejected, my own thoughts, and the list goes on and on. We want to protect our babies and help deliver others from this type of life style. I won't make excuses for my past, however, I am extremely grateful for what God allowed so I can write this book.

A thought that continued to ring in my heart as a child was "You can't go so low that God can't find you," and sometimes I really tried to go LOW.

Sometimes you don't look, smell or act like others and you feel like an outcast, but God will find you like a needle in a haystack and He'll send someone to get you. You might feel like you are ugly, fat, skinny, poor, simply off the radar, but to God you are fearfully and wonderfully made by Him. (Psalm 139:14)

Here is a question to use as a thought, do we initiate our own salvation or does this call come from God? Paul wrote to Timothy about who it is that grants repentance; we or God? In 2 Timothy 2:25, Paul answers that by writing "God may perhaps grant them repentance leading to a knowledge of the truth." Earlier, Paul asked the church at Rome the rhetorical question; don't you know "that God's kindness is meant to lead you to repentance?" (Romans 2:4 KJV) Jesus reminded the disciples that "You did not choose me, but I chose you and appointed you that you should go and bear fruit and that your fruit should abide, so that whatever you ask the Father in my name, he may give it to you," (John 15:16 KJV) and perhaps as a way to keep them humbled, having the proper perspective as to Who did the saving, and hint; it wasn't from us. (Ephesians 2:8-9 KJV) Jesus also said, "No one can come to me unless the Father who sent me draws him. And I will raise him up on the last days (John 6:44 KJV), and "<u>no one</u>" is universal in the Greek language which means neither male nor female can possibly come to Jesus unless the Father draws him (or her). The Greek word for "draw" is more profound in the Greek ("helkō") and actually means "to drag, to draw," and "to impel" and was the same word used when Paul and Silas were "dragged" ("helkō") into the marketplace for a quick trial and punishment (Acts 16:16-40). It expresses an urgency, or an insistence.

(Please use these areas to journal your thoughts)

____

____

____

____

____

____

____

____

____

____

____

33

____

____

____

<u>"Is this your gift? If not, keep reading."</u>

Chapter Nine

"Jesus the Pastor"

The PASTOR – A Shepherd, (Greek: Poimen) One who instructs, teaches, and protects. One who has compassion for, to feed the flock of God.

On the spiritual hand (Thumb: Apostle, Pointer: Prophet, Middle: Evangelist, Ring: Pastor, Pinky: Teacher).

Let's discuss the Pastor, one who cares for, protects, and also has an overwhelming compassion for others. Their objective is to feed all those who need. Pastors have an inner desire to make sure everyone is doing well. It grieves their heart to see others in trouble, loss, hungry. Jesus THE PASTOR, cares about us, His compassion has no end. (For example in what you see while they are children, Susie won't go to bed until she knows her sisters and brothers are okay. She brings other children in from the neighborhood to feed them, clothe them, bandage their wounds, etc. You will see Susie putting bandages on her doll babies or pets, even stuffed animals.)

You start to see signs that your child operates in this Ascension gift at a very young age because this area of gifting operates with an extreme amount of visible LOVE. Your child will do a lot of watching. You will turn around and see your child's eyes staring up at you after experiencing an argument, being upset, hurt, or confusion. You will see their eyes are full of compassion, looking up at you with the wisdom of the world at such a young age. In their little minds, they are trying to figure how they can help make things better. You on the other hand are trying to figure out how they could even feel this level of pain. It's in them. Consequently they are the ones who experience a great deal of pain from rejection, disappointments, fear, (I find that where you are gifted the most you experience the challenge the most to set that gift free) and that's due to their overwhelming heart (BIG HEART).

(Please use these areas to journal your thoughts)

<u>**Questionnaire that you can share with your child and please also review for yourself:**</u>

Ask them do they know that Jesus LOVES them? Get an answer.

Based on what you put in them they will be able to give you an answer from the heart of a child. We should begin early sharing with them the GOSPEL. "Jesus Christ is our Savior, he came to us to save us from a life of sin and to give us eternal life." (John 3:16) Teaching them basically how much Jesus Loves Us.

Ask them do they LOVE Jesus? Get an answer.

Ask them, What does it mean to love Jesus or to love others? Get an answer.

Why do you want to help people? Get an answer.

What is your passion? (what do you love to do?) Get an answer.

Do you like to read your Bible? Get an answer.

____

____

____

____

____

____

____

____

____

____

____

____

____

"Is this your gift? If not, keep reading."

Chapter Ten

"Jesus the Teacher"

The TEACHER – One who is qualified to effectively communicate the truths of the Bible to others. One who is gifted in illumination.

Ability to Teach: They are given the ability, skill, talent, (spiritual gift) to explain to others. (Exodus 35:34, Matthew 23:34, Ephesians 4:11-12).

Signs you were created to be a teacher:

Passionate about learning

Face challenges head on

Always seeing the glass half full

Flexibility is a strong suit

Fascinated about different subjects

Not challenged by long hours

Very creative

It concerns you when others struggle to learn

Many children at a very young age love to lead. You will find your child in a room full of children giving instructions and having a desire that others would pay attention to them. They are born leaders. They always want to play teacher as a child. Give them the chalk and board and watch them go to work. You'll find them surrounded with their baby dolls or G I Joe men giving instructions or reading to them. Teachers are special because they are given to detail and have a sincere desire to see others learning, evolving and growing. (They just want you to get it!!!)

Titus 2:7-8

"In everything set them an example by doing what is good. In your teaching show integrity, seriousness and soundness of speech that cannot be condemned, so that those who oppose you may be ashamed because they have nothing bad to say about us."

Ezra 7:6

"...this Ezra came up from Babylon. He was a teacher well versed in the Law of Moses, which the LORD, the God of Israel, had given. The king had granted him everything he asked, for the hand of the LORD his God was on him."

"Teachers who love teaching, teach children to love learning."

(Please use these areas to journal your thoughts)

____

____

____

____

____

<u>"Is this your gift? If not, keep reading."</u>

<u>**Please remember, you are gifted, you are talented, and you are special. You have been handpicked and designed by the Potter Himself.**</u>

This is my sincere thought and it is this "You will never be happy, satisfied, complete or fulfilled until you come to an AGREEMENT with GOD concerning who HE called you to BE. Agree with God, and be at peace; thereby good will come to you. (Job 22:21 KJV) Stop running, stop fighting with God. You can't win against the one who created you. "It is the Father's good pleasure to give you the kingdom." (Luke 12:32 KJV)

Remember, whom God has called you to BE, the enemy will fight at all cost for you to miss it. If you consider your ways, you really ALREADY KNOW that you were always meant to be GREAT and to represent Christ in the earth in every capacity of your life. Inside the church building and outside while using the entire person you are destined to BE.

Chapter Eleven

<u>**Misconceptions of the five-fold gifts**</u>.

Everyone knows exactly where they are and what their gifts are.

This is so Not True. So many of us later on in life still don't have a clue as to who we are and what our gifts are. It sometimes takes some training, paying attention, hunger, desires to be fulfilled to push us into our BE.

"There will come a time when you are completely tired of going around that mountain so many times and **YES** will be your answer."

I can only operate in one gifting.

The awesome explanation is like our Lord and Savior, you will find that the gifts inside of you will manifest depending on the situations and circumstances we find ourselves in. We are more like Christ than we realize. Today you might operate in your Prophetic gift and next week you will find that the Pastoral gift is in operation.

What I am praying as we go through this manuscript is that we will be yielded to the Holy Spirit and make ourselves available to be used by GOD. "The earth is groaning waiting for the manifestations of the Sons of God." (Romans 8:19 KJV)

Heretofore ~

Mirrors of Your Gift

<u>Apostle</u> – False Leaders, Hypocrites, Narcissist behaviors,

<u>Prophet</u> – Soothsayers, Liars, Witches, Tarot Card Readers.

<u>Evangelist</u> – Those who know the truth but deny the power thereof, One who preaches for filthy lucre,

<u>Pastor</u> – One who's Love is pierced with hatred, selfishness, no care or concern for others.

<u>Teacher</u> – One who instructs in untruth

<u>Definition of TRUTH</u>: A fact or belief that is accepted as true. "God's Truth" Jesus saith unto him, I am the way, the TRUTH, and the life: no man cometh unto the Father, but by me. (John 4:6 KJV)

(Please use these areas to journal your thoughts)

____

____

____

____

____

____

____

Please remember that your Gifts are yours and everyone has their own. No one can do what God has purposed for YOU to do. There are no duplicates, we are a Designer's Original.

When you decide to sit on your gifts or take on the false announcement that your gifts are not valuable, you have now left others vulnerable. Unfortunately, you have opened up opportunity for the enemy to mislead them because we have become selfish about our own trials or processes.

You are Important to the Kingdom of God and when we don't show up someone else just might not make it.

I ENCOURAGE you to MOVE forward with confidence in the Word of God (HOLY BIBLE) that reminds us "No weapon formed against us shall prosper, and every tongue that rises up against us in judgement shall be condemned. This is the heritage of the Children of the Lord and his Righteousness is of ME says the LORD." (Isaiah 54:17 KJV)

Here is another nugget before I finish; Take great efforts to keep your mind on God. The enemy would love to have your mind scattered, BUT the Bible says "Thou will keep him in Perfect Peace, whose mind is stayed on thee: because he trusts in thee. (Isaiah 26:3 KJV)

<u>**Scriptures to Remember (KJV)**</u>

Assuredly, I say to you, whoever does not receive the kingdom of God as a little child will by no means enter it."
Mark 10:15

"Before I formed you in the belly I knew you; and before you came forth out of the womb I sanctified you, and I ordained you a prophet unto the nations."
Jeremiah 1:5

"I would have fainted unless I had BELIEVED that I would see the Goodness of the Lord in the land of the living; wait on the LORD; be of good courage, and He shall strengthen thine heart. Wait, I say, on the LORD!"
Psalm 27:13-14

"For I know the thoughts that I think toward you, saith the LORD, thoughts of peace, and not of evil, to give you an expected end."
Jeremiah 29:11

"We are troubled on every side, yet not distressed; we are perplexed, but not in despair; Persecuted, but not forsaken; cast down, but not destroyed; Always bearing about in the body the dying of the Lord Jesus, that the life also of Jesus might be made manifest in our body."
2 Corinthians 4:8-10

And the Lord said, Simon, Simon, behold, Satan hath desired to have you, that he may sift you as wheat, but I have prayed for thee that thy faith fail not, and when thou art converted, strengthen thy brethren.
Luke 22:31-32

"Yet in all these things we are more than conquerors through Him who loved us. For I am persuaded that neither death nor life, nor angels nor principalities nor powers, nor things present nor things to come, nor height nor depth, nor any other created thing, shall be able to separate us from the love of God which is in Christ Jesus our Lord."
Romans 8:37-28

"For God so loved the world that he gave his only begotten Son, that whosoever believeth in him should not perish, but have everlasting life. For God sent not his Son into the world to condemn the world; but that the world through him might be saved."
John 3:16-17

"Who hath saved us, and called us with an holy calling, not according to our works, but according to his own purpose and grace, which was given us in Christ Jesus before the world began, But is now made manifest by the appearing of our Savior Jesus Christ, who hath abolished death, and hath brought life and immortality to light through the gospel:"
2 Timothy 1:9-10

But Jesus called them **unto** him, and said, **suffer little children to come unto me**, and forbid them not: for of such is the kingdom of God. Verily I say **unto** you, whosoever shall not receive the kingdom of God as a **little child** shall in no wise enter therein.
Matthew 19:14

Put on the whole armor of God that ye may be able to stand against the wiles of the devil. For we wrestle not against flesh and blood, but against principalities, against powers,

against the rulers of the darkness of this world, against spiritual wickedness in high places.
Ephesians 6:11-12

Use this area to write down a few of your favorite scriptures.

____

____

____

____

____

____

____

____

____

____

____

____

www.ingramcontent.com/pod-product-compliance
Lightning Source LLC
Chambersburg PA
CBHW052128150726
48002CB00006B/2520